Exit Moonshine, Enter Wall

Rodney Phillips

chax press 2012

ISBN 978 0925904 94 2

Printed in the United States of America

Acknowledgments are included with the "Notes" in the last pages of this book.

Chax Press
411 N 7th Ave Ste 103
Tucson, AZ 85705-8388
USA

Contents

Little Creatures

Untitled *(Radio de dream)*
Queen of Scots
Rude Mechanical
Untitled (potential Daybed)
Aquarium
Cartier Jeep
Besoin de Need & Genealogical Rhapsody
Ornaments of the Red Professors
Dayjob
Carton of Milk
Geek Schemers, Save the Robots

Modern People

Mustardseed attending
Peasblossom content
Moth amused
Cobweb akimbo
Speck pecked
Hammersmith, the end

My Girls

Yesterday I told my girls, I told them, if somebody inter-
esting talks to you, you say a few things too. You might
as well breathe at the same time and let the words out in
the air. Don't just ask questions. Give things away. Give
yourself away.

— author unknown, per Lucie Brock-Broido

Untitled for now (after Sir Thomas Wyatt)

Some fellows there are, which still bing cherries
love. Toward the moon they fly for not a reason other
than light offends them and what then, then what?
O live by night, play 'round in higher fires then,
look then again against the finest tourist's time
while tripping through the views, the cascabels abutt.
Yet do I say some things I wish I wouldn't say, and
whisker ace to face is best, but spoons are herely there
and providence is out when needed to be best. To
tickle seems a lot of precious time. Fix to the knee
caps, a type of father feather flying now, and then. Pix
and dear practicality cause havoc and pry loose the
time crime from restrictions. cage at hand.
Be baleful oh eye, when fate cries rivers, up, along
the line, the carneo dies a pink carnation yet. A lawn
goes loping into lakes, and then what cozy dine.

Travels without end (energy)

after Pierre Reverdy

The same rosebush is discovered in your prayers
that reproved us so and forever
the first ones came,   the birds
                    and then no more.

The road which was made compatible
                    two by two
is disappearing in the marching
                    rhythm above the hard stones.

Next to the fireflies they were arrested.
Next to the water they were destroyed.
their feet lifted like gunpowder
and a cloak was thrown over the light.

Those who can fly
were sold into the desert
and to maintain itself the sky opened
They are searching yet at the bottom
of the world.
The wind which they possess continues
its rounds
The door refuses
a black door.

Untitled (after Ignatius Loyola a little)

Occasionally a
body will fly with no notion
of transgression, but only
considering inspiration. And then
the secrets would be out apparently.
The uselessness of details, see
how they are appropriated and
to some general good
ascribed. Unlike how being
is, while in Saskatoon perhaps
polymorphous behaviour is probably
restrained, supra.
Deferral is another prickly strategy.
Precision is not always a pleasure,
either. Consider the refusal of
excess. Of existence the engine
is progression, one result is fratricidal.
Or boredom. The concept of transit
totally defeats ideation or identification.
Even e-business too, is spiritual.
Going astray, there are seditions
& sidelong glances, curlicues. Situated?
I am moving elsewhere to me. Into
the smile or precious cul de sac, side
bar. There is no equivalence in
romance. You must be specific.
Ambivalence and contamination are
probably necessary. Things are left
behind. Discipline is another method
unlike recreation, like trouble.
Where is the sun? The relationship
of utility to authenticity is as?
Something is not well represented.

Untitled (slightly after Federico Garcia Lorca)

Lovestruck and in the midst of it. The story of art cartoons
and arrest. Raphaelic tapestries alight the sky which wasn't
sure and the night light was trained to look the other way, as
in big philosophy, plus notions of home wizardry, um and some
may say, a weed got under them, our gallant ideas, not so
helpfully. Trite stories of body danger, of spectacles fallen by,
trunkets of gleeful abandonment, of dew disavowal, are aroused.
Flagbearer, a craze is where you are left all to yourself, no one
is bound to gether in the disappointment, which is when
the needy ones concur. But, cancion desde amor, after all,
so dark and witty, cadet, like referring to matter as spirit or
the body as soul. Disturbed twinkie, it isn't amenable so at last
and yet never, delivered, from the photo on the porch.

The Last letter to John Taylor

We got better, futuristically. Light bulbs! Isotopes
in the corner are encouraged by the famous melancholy
of Mallarme. The joyous and procedural is the tao
of not being. Whew, we are all in the wrong bodies
after all, said Eileen after she walked me home. It
seemed totally the perfect answer: Ed Asner or the Heliotrope.

The rule is, everything has to be good. Retribution
at least, is unhelpful, except in the botanical,
experimental & ornamental cases. Wild
attractions, which are inhibited reactions after
all might prefer us. Lo, the sub theme
is the unlikely appearance of friendship.
Black jack! J. Lo! It seems impossible trickery.

Fantasia on a theme by Whittier

What is so diabolical about weather and classical
music? How efficiently and with what
notable dependencies do they create lethargy,
together lulling. The birds have taken cover,
are politely hiding out, or missing in action. Everything
is pointed, uppermost and matters are too peripidous
and full of happenstance. A Chinese roof?
But in some sense, the nature of snow is all
artifice. I had no idea life was not an adventure
tale, but a political thesis entwined like so many
transcendentalists in words. Six over six seems
perfectly suited to the fiendish looking out, as if
architecture was not already whimsy. Perhaps reading
an issue of Artforum would help. We are well into
the last hours of the classic, everything conditioned
by our environment as we fall unhurriedly through
the centuries thinking: the birds must be hiding
somewhere. Fool, following finances and availability,
how can things not be romantic? Isn't this
easier than trying to explore the empyrean
on your own? You wish the name of your dog was.

F: Marie & the Petit Etymological slogans

A crib is a mechanism for cheating. See?
That's it, give them behold. Beehive them,
as crib means home, music about
the mangers: Polish and polish, Conran
and Conrad, who was dedicated to English,
not to waiting. There is a big picture, all
my breathing says this: rain also, is a process.

As in discourses on Chinese poetry:
14 poems in Cathay are not derived from
other poems, says Yunte. So attractive,
such practical garb. That is, grab
a contribution from Gertrude Stein.
A summary of this: the cards are discarded,
at bay, a transference occurs in nature, voices,
strategies drown us out, arguing:
Of the possible sentences, which is a good one?
The photography of grammar, an idyll.

Histoire et literature

Ecrive la vie ordinaire comme un ecrit l'histoire.
(Write ordinary life as though it were history)

— Flaubert, as per Jane Cooper

Not this.
What then?
      — Ron Silliman, *Tjanting*

Botanicals of Craziness

Marigold! Flower of the devil, it
can be used to keep mosquitoes and other
insects away and since I got this one
the other day, no flies! Or maybe it's
the cooler weather. I saw some heather
at the flower man's and didn't recognize
it until I got home. In Hard Times,
by Charles Dickens, Miss Pross twitches
with an affliction & consequently is always
retiring into houses. A little later I am
looking at Lily, Rose, Carnation. I think
how ivy transgresses our allegories
for boundaries. Ice plant after
dinner refreshes the too spirited. Can each
flower have a trait in this our time? A useful
property pour l'amour? The mint leaf began
speaking a long time ago. Send help
to the least of us. Randomly.

Seven of Nine

This is a poem about individualism and its enemies
or the obverse. I used to think touch was very individual
but now I'm not so sure, considering the Vivian Girls
or the Stepford wives. You know, there is a yearning
for the corporate which masquerades as individualism
and vice versa. Catholic schools, uniforms, nuns
and priests of course. What about John Gault? Purity
and discipline are hallmarks of the socialistic. How
many details can you actually have before you don't have
any, but only darkness? The Borg were the masters of corporate
feeling, and look how comfortable they seemed. Why not
develop a baroque mentality, skipping lines, sending filaments
across the abyss. Or like Walker Evans in the subway.
Such nice white socks. Ants, hills, bees, hives are all about
togetherness aren't they. The individual is an illusion then?
What about ornament, the night? How encompassing. With bad
attitudes everywhere. What about Gongora and company?
Who was the company? The general and his specifics.
The Vernacular in progression and advance, do they have
a place? Like an apartment? The Baroque is so individual.
The secret of the photostat is maximum illumination. One
thing after another, as Donald Judd would say.

Nuit de Varennes

I don't care how dark it gets as long as we can still move.

Where is the little myth we used to have?

The fruit salad will bloom on the plate like a bouquet

Fabulous ephemera. A constant force for giddy flight.

the soul is tetanous; gun barrel burnishing

this iron comfort. These reasonable tattoos,

Whoever you are. We too lie in drifts at your feet

I am so nervous of my life the little of it I can get ahold of,

fled and pursued transverse the resonant fugue

lost in a small collision of the orchids.

The Protestant Era

At the Metropolitan Community Church on the corner of 13th Street
and Seventh Avenue, which is in shrouds, the sermon this week is "The Brute
Force of Prayer." So much for the likes of Teilhard de Chardin, Bonhoffer
and Tillich. Or maybe not. The Book of Common Prayer was controversial
in its time and led to burnings, as today translations of Rumi do not. Except
 in the pages of the NYRB which are blowing across the intersection, pale wings
of vultures who have lost their ability to banter. Or wimples? Fortune and
detriment, assignation and divine designation are all ahistorical, including
 as they do a peculiarly personal view of relations and encumbrances,
like "The Pastures of Heaven," which was written by Steinbeck, whose corner
this was not, nor the Campo dei Fiori with slumbering beauts beneath it.
The subway, like the Venusian canals, can be dreamy. There is no pleasuring
oneself. Be practical! Think of a Jackie Collins novel which sits egret-like,
curling, poolside. In the fashion of the day. To meditation (in some versions)
do we owe the fact that her hero was once a woman. Far out, everyone
was, in some sense and for the time being.

A Poem ending with several unrelated lines by Byron

Who wants to be ironic and romantic at the same time?
Sentimentality and cynicism are cousins, you see,
or at least so said George Gordon, Lord Byron, afterward.
What about sincerity and lies telling the same story.
What is to be done? (this of course, like everything, has been
already written). This reminds me of, nothing. A devilish trick,
an impossible sort of semblance. Next thing you know,
the end is near. Fragility is the same thing as strength
apparently. I have no parents, and am often wanting
to be one. In some circles this would be considered
delinquent behaviour. I would to heaven that I were
so much clay. Or, Love's a capricious power, I've
known it hold out through a fever caused by its own heat.

The Literary offenses of Fenimore Cooper

They make a windex with a berry fragrance
now. This is overwhelming
evidence
of something.

Ornans seems such a funny name, eh?
It was where the senses deserted you.

The perfect career, the effigy. You better
get your references in order. Join the army
of lovers, the peek at the past.
Captivity narratives have paved your way.

Ah, the Buttes Charmante, the Bateau
Lavoire, Bain de Soleil, the Upper West Side.
Agog, really.

Nietzsche teaches someone, perhaps us, that truth is multi
farious, various and unlegendary.

It is so inflammatory
(in the good sense, of corolla and corona),
a narcotic effect of looking, Consider it a warning.

Leyendas Espanolas

It was the noche in which we were told about
Don Quijote. That he was gay. It was probably
Cervantes they were talking about. Also
there was considerable talk about what happened
after the silencing of Sor Juana. Mala noche. Nothing.
Las Meninas were wheeling thru skys, not so paltry
in pink. Soie exactly. Mole is made of something
like 12 chiles when properly prepared. We considered
the ecstasy of historical research. We will worry about
Plutocracy demain, but aujordhui the peoples. Peeps?
For a while there was la baila. or an equivalent
in chairs. And when the incidence of the Maids
exposed itself, we were cheering as if for Genet.
Grapes and parmesano citizens! La Hospitalidad de
Carmen. Somos en flor. Mentioning Granada was
eneffable until. Then.

Palais Royale

Dexterity and articulation are strange values (the extreme
friendliness of it all), as are an attendance at galas, or
undersea nightmeetings, the great disillusionment of
love and the illusions of love. Which are one and the same.

Therefore, held in place the drapery smooths itself. Sleep,
all is about sleep, desire and the battle against desire.
It is supposed to be about self-knowledge, not insouciance
and rose hips. Brother Francis? Speaking for the birds. Someone

not so normative really, had to. Its so psychological, the playful
heart in revolt, like Pascal. Only, he knew what he was up against.
As did Robespierre, Racine, Moliere, Camus and the others.
Panegyrics are a shock to intimacy and a cause sometimes

of an extreme and particular understanding of purity and
the opposite: worry, forgetfulness, disappearance.

The Birth of Sociology

Funky dogs: such as the ones that don't

dance well? The Dutchman is flying, we sing

our song. Next to nothing, bikes go backward.

Friendliness, uprightness and a little pleasure,

doing bits of research. Tricks to track. Divinity

U C has its intermittent lapses. So, the way

gets poshly lost, ecclesiastical, swanlike, debtful

of doubt. Try lining up the players. Lecture or

hike? Supreme negation of the miraculous.

Grotto of mumblings. Mumbo jumbo. Papa loves

Mambo. You are full of delinquency, even blaspheming

my tangolier, Something is before everything for sure.

Everything is coextensive too. The mysterious preludes

the oh so evident. The spirit is the body, and air is preeminent

want. A filegree of lace, ions in rosewater. Spankings,

featherwise, Accuracy, paedomaniac to the Last. Jeremiah

Field-Flowers was in big trouble at Oxford. Florisant,

a tube of cold fluorescent was born. Maybe.

Concerto

Phish. a rock band, a garbage truck comes. Up the hill, refrigerated.
So, you made a mis-identification. Identify don't compare, they both
have wheels and are made of some sort of sheet metal, nest pas? Pots
and Pans encore. Some phases of phraseology. How long is a phrase.
Is this one? Incomplete? It's better than an F. Avant, tried and true. Next
winter the demon will be kept outside, freezing. Slumbertools are
importuned, imported and chances are. More! Onward!

To the library, the free bookstore. The camp of it. The perfection de dios
and a few others. Campion chomping and a cast of the finest. Invite
the literate, a chemistry of persons, nalities, provide proof. Poof.
Up in air, Immortalizing the sincere Stratified society sucks. Sincerely,
the blazon de. Love it, ending with little conjoiners. Er, restitute. To
the last of lines.

Nineteen lines about violets

Think of it, Bezique
and the quiet noise
of perfume, L'Interdit or
Quelques Fleurs
The violet industry
of Parma was founded by
Marie Louise, the Empress
after Josephine. Looking
for electronics, one comes
upon visualizers and projectors.
Its like the desperation
of psychoanlysis, in which
we are trained to see
something that is there
after all. Abstraction
is worrisome. Traipsing
along the woody trail
at Malmaison, one ends up
tending gardens! Cancellations,
like a guillotine are averted,
in the meantime esplanade
through every last lightbulb,
like perishable monuments
or Pocatello. Dubiously
swooning? In the end,
a small red splash
on the petal, the artifice of
understanding.

Abandoned verisimilitude

Judgments and opinions in the area of art are doubtful murmurs in mental mud. Only appearances are fertile; they are gateways to the primordial. Every artist owes his existence to such mirages.

Robert Smithson. from *Incidents of Mirror Travel in the Yucatan*

Poom

Coming out
of the Guggenheim I thought
I saw Poom written on a nearby
wall. I argued with
myself for the whole subway ride
downtown, when
I wasn't busy trying
to seduce someone or the other
who was standing in front
of me. Spectacular was all
I could say to the assemblage
of riders who didn't even
notice me. Which sometimes is
a blessing. It seemed appropriate
to be captured by my dark
side then. Like the box by Cornell
with at least a dozen Caravaggios in it
which symbolizes unconquerable
desire or just a thirst
for blue boys. Tohu bohu
you know, is Hebrew for the
original state of things without
form or void, with no inside or
outside. A little like what the
Symbolists were doing, confusing
the world with the self, according
at least to Edmund Wilson.

Caribou, tea

The big old red buildings are grandeur
 itself, grandiosity incarnadine, symbolizing
the honorific satiety of the long dead
like Sappho or Eliot, George. Like knowledge
which is behind the bush, like Satraps,
ornamentalists
or beaus, whispering roads, it is
time to curtsey now,
like iron maidens, the millions
are shaking on along the roads end.
Spring is gushing up among reliquaries,
as honesties are silken.
Campus what? Zoo socks to be fashion.
Just in Sitka the spruces are gone.
Gads, them trophies too? Vanished.

Aberdeen

The older women in their thin and fiery garments
of flowers, they've never heard of lumber. Only
pine trees upholding nothing. But eventually they let go,
float free. I want them to, for love is a transitory thing,
and they do, with exasperating ease. They have no hand
hold on life, just newspapers in the basement, growing
we, meshing together as they come to know, everything
is just not everything else. The Hydrangeas engulf the
porch, blue & enormous as if metal were present, but
there was no porch. Only seconds of mistaken luxury.
Luxury, what next? Calling out names, the end. Under
clothes on the line dancing like the thin pages of
the encyclopedia, caressed, a backbone like a closet.
Mind so thick, dark and darker green.

Mackerels

Walking from Nick's on Sunday evening
the sunlight is silver on the clouds, (formal clouds:
better than gods). Mackerels, sardines. Fragrant,
like water, Singing? Some boys are yelling out loud,
speeding (up Bedford). Two of them not driving
put back their heads, and yell like the streets
were echo chambers. Perhaps they are signaling
to artists, or to the hidden life. As it
becomes darker, each smile is more welcome.
Not one eye is of chrome. All along the route
(it seemed there was a trail of) cocaine, like lost salt
But the next thing we know, we are, metamorphosed
into little flowers singing by the minute.

Chinas y Criollas

O Yes

Today I think I am answering back, framing
devices like shorter lines, or more beautiful beliefs.
Perhaps I will write a poem about furniture, the ottoman
for instance, and loneliness, young love like a cereus
lolling on a sunken patio. The episteme.
In Arizona is the desert and the largest dam, the
oldest bridge and the bluest lake, a few eyes of God.
In Arizona is a telescope, mountains, We
be on their tops. The little ants who live in
the bushes' thorns will be saving up good drops of
processed water. It will take getting used to.
The birds of paradise will be seeing, alighting
in the jaws of coyotes telling us all about how.

Comidas

This is a poem about matter and spirit, exclusively,
how they can teeter, talking about heartbrakes and spasms,
saying aloud 'What good is this, first one then the next?'
I answer myself, like an elf telling me how I should feel,
how I need to be serious about love and the rest of it.
Like Xerxes, I think of conquering and rolling in hay.
I love however, this idling and the red and yellow food,
the purple beans, neon sun, all falling over like a lock.
And I say in this tone of shyness, with totally little templates
to myself: I don't think he is coming here now, it seems
after all that there are no eyes really jumping, rolling up
like three cherries. I am way too tired to be serious, but wary.
This is no poem about loving. Though really, we are for it.

Head in the Clouds

However affections can surprise us they do,
turning one thing, a tattoo farm for instance, into
another, and in one instant after an introduction
has been obtained. Looking is not that simple.
It does not evince sweetness, a quality much
overvalued these days, found everywhere, even
in graceless walks and awkward reputations.
One must learn distracted observation of cows
on a hillside. The love life is concerned, for instance,
not with lack of heaven, just with regular cows, those
with the black and white spills on them. And
beneath them the grass, emerald green. Emeralds
are not a bit like grass, not single-minded
and obsessed with one thing, like the body,
as if there was one. And so
the reverse is eventually true: telescope,
sleepmate, microscope, mirror. This can be done
to any number of characters, the fire lighting up the sky
the emerald curtain, slight rose. Atomic eyes,
hole in the chest, Starships---

Playground

When I went to visit John's loft on Thanksgiving I
noticed some brown construction paper was covering
his beautiful windows and that a star was sitting on
the floor. In one corner was a nest of tissue, crumpled
up with pieces of mirror nestled in the folds. There is
nothing better than looking sometimes. Dazzled by art
and friendship I feel there is something about trust that
might disable me, like too many blues singers with no
betdtime stories, like no rose movies, no pink cactus land
ever did. No one however, is fallen in the mud like a wreck.
Or pretending to be born in Connecticut. Picturesque views
are still stalking us, we go wondering if the big dog is ever
gonna come. I wonder how olive trees assimilate the style
of willows, and just who is after who. Ant after ant is
crawling around in the rain. Experts are after them.

The Dream of Lana Turner again

Here I sit waiting to be discovered as if
this street in P Town was Schraffts. The dogs
go by and each one looks at me. The choices
are writing about morning, or the air or
the sun which is coming up over that roof,
gable or cupola. It's trying to get at me. One
of those slight little birds in the air makes
a sound, supposedly like a hinge, but he's
not really up yet. Another little cheep is just
too happy to be believed. I am reminded
of the ache, which is not relieved by sleep
the way you think it would be,
for someone to wake up with, which if
I had, I would now be missing this
morning. Chagrin. It is recognition's
sneakiness I regret. Epiphanies are saying
awaken, or is that the sun? The so called
catastrophe of the dark is covered over.
There is a fat low yew and three
companionable teenage birches, all of
them dappled by the source of life.
Suddenly, I am seized with the need
to make a map of this place like Charles
Olson did of Gloucester. Or Francis
Bacon, from whom I did not learn this
coping strategy. A tiny L-shaped
house is three steps down from a park
ing lot. Other houses on Arch Street
are also on Pearl and Johnson Streets
since it really just an alley. Pity some
houses were built upon yards or gardens.
Yet, the old falling down Portuguese
house sidles up cozy to the trendy
seventies number, exuberantly with
inside paneling on the out.

Lipstick for Halloween

I was getting dizzy with excitement when Caroline
mentioned the lipstick episode of the night before
and how much it bothered her. The thing was that,
suddenly all the boys wanted to use her lipstick
which was very red and because it was Halloween.
Frank, for instance, started it because he was dressed
like Mozart, or Harpo Marx. Caroline didn't
like the fact that he had a cold or something,
and had been upstairs for the entire first part,
except for dinner. I think it was okay
for Nick to use the lipstick, he was dressed up
like Marie. Well he wasn't at all, but his mannerisms
were mimicking her way of standing up straight with
her arms crossed like she was holding herself. Tight.
She said: "now that's my kind of man" when John
finally came out dressed like a dirty gas station attendant
with long hair. Well, mine too. Doug, the guy who
earlier had put paper towels in the candle holders which
were too large for the candles and set everything on fire
was looking like Cynthia Ozick. Or Cynthia Ozick on
drugs. Someone else we didn't know was covered
in nets, saying something like "I've been a naughty boy."
So had everyone. Everywhere. So, as I was
saying, I was crazy with hope, and then I wasn't.

Nightgown

My dead are down where all the hippy headed kick especially,
and write Tree Trunk in their diaries. Moonlight eats the medium
on the dock and leaves no leftovers, saving love for last, loose.
Boy in the boo park is next to the manchild. Run. Be any color
you can sing Toucan, so why so preposterly pee? Plagues have had
me, dew has not. Martians, red folk are, me. Capitals of pain are
lo Lobelias. Ishmael transmogrify I. Space fills with feuilltons,
sparrow are make sense. duneworms go riderslarking. Knowledge
of. They believe nothing of that sort. They are immune to beliefs.
Everyone preserves a main chance even lovers who tank leaders,
we scuff their shoes, careening thee case best last. Flower power
pots transparently flush, am core, am belly. Washing machines are
prisoners which we wingover, practically absent from our time/
temps. And its great partnerspace, brother sleep too touchy.
Absence axus. Messengers withworn eyes whistle us. Drink
despair. Bodies of the blessed, taletellers of the best, pink punks
with platitudes—Danger is our sister, she clears our ears of
ribaldry, she demands a vacance. A mouth a purse a winesoaked
mop flies, classless, demotically are we. Perspiration is personal,
modesty what never one ever vied, ear.

Little Creatures

Significant literary effectiveness can come into being only in a strict alternation between action and writing; it must nurture the inconspicuous forms that fit its influence in active communities better than does the pretentious universal gesture of the book—in leaflets, brochures, articles and placards. Only this prompt language shows itself actively equal to the moment.

— Walter Benjamin

Untitled (Radio de Dream)

Whose fault might all be anyway? Twilight men,
the jai-alai players, sayers of little lullys, or trini loops lapidaries,
all frulli y canta or musto trinkiets, play putanesca frankincense
trippin over rusty ruffies, aka little foxes. Nix no. Terriers next,
aargh says vu plupe. Yon soldier has a tree like attitude
& is named Marquis or Dubuffet perchance. Protractor, ginny flack
oboeys, tracking mite breath to cosy fog o want. Delire de fanciness,
cambio min irrational desespoir. Flank after flank, Here Kitty, aloha
along the vie. Pastan letters or Pasternak, you there, cantankerous
transversion, ringlet and tricot, m reading and peril, opportunity mongrel,
hybrid if poorest o panics, ice lies, die trying. Hats? on bicicleta?
Devotions are graven. Carmelites gone, trying escalators. To each echo of
cludy, neonumental heart sickness, als fratori minores, picking up lint, each
piece a wordy world type of the the art. Craftiness Mon. A la Maui
de Empire, trust isn't hereabouts hid. Hoop hoop, don't make quite that
vigored a timbre. To be fragile again. Dream put etre. You
daisy, you---fluctitious fructose pance. I mogrify every momen
ayur being in expanse. Philological beat raub. Seele in raume. Fly
true the air, whish, vent au vole, vent a tripletop tree, flutter, graze, skim.
Sin past all enciphering. Fu, the later flutterby, mancion eee
iii, left, right, leff, leff. Majexty, calling. Reality a carp swimming
pool, or a dam Ned crewel finial on a stairway. Tread on.

Queen of Scots

with Winthrop. and his basket bases
thinking in French. & past participle
oh we. wallflower.   wainscot
I haven't any. sight. site
vocally said: agave, Ogilvy. O.
flicker confiture; flute & publicity
truth being imageless. no matter
petals designed for empathy, telepathically
I am knowing. all about. folding
a feint notice. origination is not destiny
waif, wayfarer, with every gain a stranger
subjectivity. of sexuality. lily uncalled
for. come near. let go. Advertisement.

Rude Mechanical

Discover educations, elation, study and research
the fine liens, so we all might go altogether, all go
together. Strings, like a guitar, notational of
the daily things with collateral abundance of ideas
and systems to express them. Develop me into
someone like Eliot Ness. Protractor man, elevator to
where we don't know, its cloudy like Tiepolo,
glowing. The worst thing is that.
There is no answer, and that is the answer. There
has never been any answer. So what. Corona
del Mar! Toward the anachronism of the faithful
we march. My focus is out, the dreds are whipping.
Travel on, we got to travel. This is the place where I
was. Purpose: transcendence and immanence. Potencies
and princelings all to themselves. Both lack a
certain love for roses, Mohammed however, mentions
them everywhere as he tells us: The world
is a translation of the heavenly.

Untitled (potential daybed)
       — *"legerdemain in the Elaboratory"*
              Ronald Johnson (ARK 72) —

Now, what do you want to do about frankincense,
patchouli oil or vetiver, all tools of Satan, decriminalized
nonetheless and disguised as glassy liquids of desuetude?
Also, the loved one is appearing as a big Harlequin
great dane. Lovely dark guy. Doesn't slobber either. Like
some I know. Pines, vale of heavenly rest, all. Yikes, rest?

Lay down and dream we have been intersecting all along
as if there is no help for it. Melpomene for instance is dancing
on our noses. Fractured toe of hers don't help much though.
Porticules, curly cues, pool cues, actor signs, boots: all blew
up in a big cool Flaubertian lack of distance. You know
blah blah blah, c'est moi. Dillinger, Rimbaud? Especially if.

What is modernity? Can I read to you from the first Iris
Murdoch novel? Potential daybed, that one. It's all over anyway,
Peak Freens and Dentyne stuck in the hair. Frangipani, I am
tempted to think, is an oil too. Echo things nosewise. Rosewater
burns the eyes apparently. Things don't come together so
well. Swelling sense of direness zips u up, gordo. Funny name
for a dog, twirling in the starry eye.

Aquarium

There are no principles of literary history just figures
of thought. Baroque and rococo at the best. Flying
 fish and pancakes tomorrow! Lets give lectures to
the other places in town. Cast them out into utter mush,
the Outer Cape, moonpies and all? Mushroom soup and flags.
There is a beach called Flagler, near one of the cheapest places
to live in the world, or Florida. I am pressing on, claiming
county after county for an imaginary land. Sweet dreams
and illusory whitenesses. It is a picket after all, on
the line with the boys, unhappy---well you can be unhappy
alone. I say to that: union busting again. Bargains
like frizzy lettuce at Filenes? Beelzeebub!
Bub? like a friendly fry. Smite thee my factitious arrangement
of thought. Yellow fin tuna serves as the balance here.
Particles, ah, particles….dust motes, bunnies, bombs
feel free to flee to their house. Whose, the house of Art?
In the arctic circle it is easier than Antarctica. We might
never know, this and many other things, so, back to the French stuff,
such as art history. Or is that German, as in Wincklemann and
his agonistic families? Familigia for it. Bowl of mooses. Mosses?
Must mangy times communally come up? Hide in the food,
woods or the grocery store. Celery is like trees. Weather too.
Check out pain. Trusty feel down the woops, leg. Alliance is not
the same as dalliance, worlds apart. Pret a porter. Helios
come down here now. We fractured us. Samba time this semana,
slumbering, so sincerely, trout mouth. Fable and not. Gold
dust, twins, twinkies, dry mouth fatigue at last. Out of trouble.
At last. The flight of someone turned to wood, Daphne, Chloe,
Perseus, Gorgon, pale butterfly. Orange Roughy. Wickedness
is endlessly defeated by good. Except.

Cartier Jeep

Is the self really all that permeable and what
does that mean, anyway? Ah, an identity meditation.
It is ok to be enjoying attention and company, this
wacky time. Bite me, says who? Bus boys aren't

on busses, you know. Such innate wisdom.
You are so full of character, with chintzy cult eye
brows. Like Cesar Vallejo, like Dada, charged with
particles, dirty girl. As it happens though no one

here really is a girl now. Listen to the machinery.
The are no constituencies anymore, really.
Lamentable. Chinese war lords, green plastic shelves
and rockets, donkey rocket merengue. Are you a

line from C's poem? You know the purpose
of local radio stations, to make you feel good
about where you live, instead of New York. Or
to sell pick up trucks. Pleasures only detour us,

and not to be oneself only, is a bummer. You
can't be saying things like I need you so, that's
just a song. Chance makes everything blue too
just like an orgone box. Virtue equals contingency,

pretence?. Then someone was asking about the afterlife
of the piece with the site specific situation. As if
Judge Crater was young, not lost, a gestural idea. Oh no,
we won't have any of that Renaissance humanism here.

Besoin de Need & Genealogical Rhapsody

The luscious sideways crawling up the wall carpet
of the starflowers, is pale and disastrous
to some. Also the tale
about the mountains of southern China looking just like
the paintings of the masters,

Yikes. What about how "Views" of things and picturesque places,
especially in Italy, Bomarzo being.

Luckily some can transcend memories, the tragedy for instance
of the past of the excellent Greek poet, Yannis Ritsos
who ended a poem with "Thank you, my love."

Such unmercantile attitudes. Ah wilderness,
a title already taken so you can't.
It's the legacies of the classical, how

all these women on Memorial Day look like cute
young boys, well, at least some of them.
Exquisite would be a word to use, as this requires some
intelligence, pluperfect professor, happening eclogues.

Imaginary philosopher, there are
too many roadblocks, between one and another
for love to ever prosper, which viewpoint is called,
the billiard table theory of life. Like
the river rushing, which allows us to hang on to
the watercress for just a minute. Next time —

He said he had a little bit too much *besoin de* need.

Ornaments of the Red Professors

What are we to do when we learn
that the hero of The Red and The Black
is a manipulative young stud? What about
seeing domestic photographs of sweet
illicit perversion? Oh what about the ballet,
or Night Fishing in Antibes? Ci-devant
marketing has ravished us. Who is Aggie
Gund after all, I thought perhaps of the famous
stuffed animals. Woops, there are more
dogs in the poem now, dachshunds.
On a stroll in Mayfair in 1813 when
The Corsair and Mansfield Park were
published. No repenting hand waves,
no chlorophyll, languor held in check,
just. Voluptuaries and eccentrics are both
poised and shy in front of the immensities.
The poor wolves are hunted by everyone,
including the Irish wolfhound after all.
No dogs have occupations, really, anymore.
Greyhounds at 45 miles per hour can
catch up to gazelles. The passionate infat
uation of one human being for another
is only one kind of love, according at least
to Aristotle and his Nichomachean Ethics.
Sincerity, the inner light and a dedication
to the ideal were probably values that came
later. Eve Sedgwick typed out the first
45 pages of Sodom and Gomorrah, volume
4 of Proust, so she would have a more
intimate encounter with this famous scene.
This is a prime example of polyvocal textuality,
or a charivari, a pilgrimage to other places
which is, of course, the joy of literature.
Taking pleasure in the deferral of synthesis
I wonder if synthesis is always such a pleasure,
or if that is beside the point. We and Shakespeare

know about the foolishness of theatrical poses,
as disguising the secret of agency. Others,
as noted, are obsessed with naturalism,
and garden ornaments for instance tires
or upset bathtubs. This is not the sad story
of Matthiessen or Arvin, but a triumphal
march of mysterious character. And also
the opportunity to be misunderstood.
Storytelling is the supreme skeleton of
conceptual art. At least we are left alone,
considering the few talks about imitation,
or mimicry we decried.

Dayjob

You should be a tree trunk, you are so
manly. You haven't even seen. I like
delicate people, or at least people who
appear. No one here is to be confused
with a locomotive. Except the blond who
has on boxers. It is as if watching him
carefully, the drifting icebergs are
put asunder. Caffard! The end of fiction
and the mixing up of the genres is like
a transcontinental meeting. The Golden
Spike! In our histoire de perfection, we
include some lesser lights. Comparison is the
last thing to do, but. Did you know that
Mohammed wore a rose around his
neck? Now, that is something
surprising and explains the patterns
in the carpets. Who
was it that believed in conciliations like
that? Silly conjunctions of containment.
Oh, shit, too many C words. We are
striving to introduce this sort of thing
into our motorcourts. Timely translation for
instance, of this and that metaphysical
stance. What is the spiritual about? Say,
is that the fire of forgetfulness I see you
hanging with? The gardens were left
struggling alongside the strada, the boul
evard. Hausmann the devil, or the true
secrets of skateboarding, all the same.
Won't the prescription take care of that
last doubt around Buddha? The tree
is way too portly for our cause, or the
particular necessity of enlightenment.

Carton of Milk

Everyone here watches television
or rents movies, which is only one step
toward urteilkraft. Turning the pages is lolling,
lifting veil, consistent & handmaidenly, doubtful
about lotus accidents curling the flower footed,
saying: what joins is inexplicable, and alternating
and variable, this striking conception is as
frightened as radiation, as spitlight as the sens of living
in a capsule, granular and not inexhaustible. Sight below.
The tricking & disbanding, named circuitous nights
of love, lets. Chirographic features are like spirits sweeping
geographically into vials of safety as if they needed help.
The paint and the image are consistently confused, if
that's not possible, ideas and concepts. Lest the abstract
part of it. Sit, conehead beside the master, mister if you
hear voices, paramount to sanity or too near derangement,
aberration, sit: each method & particularity pleases too, like
an easel, weighs how side swipes. Occurs an accordian.

An envy fought by sitting is still or petrified. Leaking
misgivings bout terror and prayer, of mind is the
heart the capital, motors switch like the water under
foot wishes an aesthetic coincidence. In pen and pencil
then streetwalking to clue central ascendancy, liberty
enjoining yet against the night, portable, capable
structures of weed, possibility. Interruption the goddess
of twisted lip, out to dry or flee, a faborite suburb:
ranch house, portly flamingo, egrets Mitty, place of Mars
of tenty tender, hole of night, ephemera skidding
upon lunacy. Instead of singular plants: specimens hortatory.
Prideful dissemblance is left against normalizing heat it is
troubling & imperfect understanding, nite.

Disengagement, or

King of the duotones, splint sliver in tangibility
to proper places and prototypical hideaways
of the Tokugawa period. Hollyhocks. More
of it and trails to secret bins. Bottle of, Chanel!
Big and clear. Golden Lysistrata say, need and
syringes, the top is loose again. Treatment
is necessitated: X Cam, oats and mares both.
torque at the momento. Root vegetables
simper like they. Oz this and all. But not
in the magazine. In the very fire. Wing ding
is a sort of comeuppance, or condescenscion
or giving up of some sort. Offeratory
and buscamantine like a church of the period.
Heian? To say nothing of the blanc prideux,
I mean to say. Eleve and the twentynine poems.
Swimmy all over the places of suck decline,
saved. Not by but from. Circle line goo,
aren't to say. This is the 17th Century or
earlier, a baroque rondel. A cheese,
a window pain, a cousine to a lunette. A
Alack, and more. Whilomville visited and
the other places. The eerie savings. Prod
uctivity italienne, no plastic resolution, wired.
Cop and nickie lines. Flargrant pints of funny
stuff. Wyandotte or Wickenberg? Or some
palace to hide. A diner, garage mechanical,
a portent and whip. Do dah. Free us from.

Geek schemers, save the Robots!

Someone is shedding their semblance, becoming air.
Or au pair. On these woodland paths? Mr. Washington
Irving for instance, was so attracted to waterfalls
and other misty scenes, shaggy trees, air ferns &
anti-macassars or moccasins. Ah yes the Deerslayer
is saving the girlies in his canoe, keenly and partly this
is a diagram, or maybe a diadem. How never
necessary is communication. What about then
our essential loneliness? Like playback and the
neighbor dreading a diet of documentation. My neigh
bor doesn't have no horse. I'm not that flexible.
So sensitive to the not ineffable, like the birth
of landscape painting in China for instance. What
about some mystic decoration, that don't
symbolize anything anyway, the allegory is
nowdays a narrative, art is the exclusion, the
levitation of scholars. In an attempt to
curry favor I have now noticed that it was Cooper
after all. What things are in a playbook? How not
to lurk, oneself, a modern verse translation. Excess
is inaccessible, too late the Salem witches are exonerated,
just like the Hardy Boys or Nancy Drew. Maybe you
should ration your TV? It is good to be doing secret things
in public. But now, like Dickens, a last chapter is needed
on the blooming.

Modern People

Nay, cake. Item, 'a face.' See mock hate row, a ray gain.
All assume men noon. New 'tis a paw stick a mate in aways, say?

Hera, am I to get out a male, I upright the less so?
Aid a gay toy, Kay. Fall, ache at a new. So am I. Up prop a poet, Ace.

— David Melnick, *Men in Aida*

Mustardseed, attending

we don't know who is capable, we don't know nothing,
sizerains of sagesse we aint. a(m)men/able, destitute, arable.
we canaan think a thing, materialism enjoins us to statutory
fantasias we communicate, obliterates the penury of true

preparator for statuary, we find reasoning craqueliaried
in peachblossom blue. sins, phonies and pale pituitary liens,
we oculate them, treats seeing eye puppies to fat plovery.
we abate, we stir ourselves up, we satiate. plentitude bounds.

we don't get easier, placating triflery, phantastique wifery ay
the miens rus, we tree posses and we bee phylacteries intent
we cinder to die, we arabesque in capitals, we Granada free
with fabled coquetry, semiotica's recense and recompensery

decline us. evergreen, at the Alhambra, we leonine to popery
almost we triple tree. we mint. hot hostelry we gwan be fine.
no swan. flo boat. Oklahoma. she almost resuscitate three
of are kind. occasionally our occasion eventuallies. alley allies.

Peasblossom content

Lutetia! Home of La & Faberge eggs in exile,
casita de mis fortunas, frajeel tracery, luciercery
swirly, twirl scent Oblossoms. Demain, Magwitch:
Fledgling franks, twittering like fleur-de-lis tree.

Cri, uselessness ice practiced, servante a maniere,
balcone, from it fly the fevered delicacies, whee.
Maids, Republic, widen yourself, flee niche & lily
pastefloriferous to the easy fee of gender, mentate

fey harlequin, kink devotee, shaved triumphally ji.
Text time bleets outre he robust in favor of. Oh esse,
always, teatime, zine-splashers, autre ghoat, Dime.
Plasir de soie, rubythroat, turquoise desesperent.

Argyll, lordly possibilities, me gowns deranged
recombinantly, Riviera, foster siblings a la languour.
Banan Fosters! Rouge, rouge, rogue destinee, la!
Laid out circuitry delicieux, Canasta, bon temps.

Fortuitous bibelot, Saracen adornments de troop,
secret mimicry, mime mystically Madeleine glorioso.
La bec fin, peristaltic at last, ornamental topography
Assyrian fiends devote us the frivolitous dementation.

Pascal, we commiserate, filigree sussurate, embassied
to the felicitous. True Frangipani, or the pink, exhilirate,
sentences, oracule, hortatory y didactic in topology, sew
recommence Tamar to morrow, up upon tumbley autumn.

Moth amused

Afflatus of engninery, divina vocabule, Portia generates
a cloud of soul, silkiness developes plenary hypnocracy
we emuliate or betterment to congratule a miniscule
of Caroline. Euphrates Piscatory. Hen finery is on tour, C.

vain vanity we mirror Wegee evenfully. Congeals loverly on
our congoleum, consequently immoderately resigned are
we. Plea after Plea, Plie. Ex cathedra is usefully dude
like and characteristical charismatical felt near to fieldom.

Fiefs and drums. Platoons of boony . . .Basta my Tonto.
Circule and Decembrist, revolute to prostitute Oronokoo
and his(her) friends, in the manner of Miss Rosa, soul sol
iloquy of heartrent bent feelies sent soi-mysteriously sigh

ing flew the aire. Compton, Conrad, Consald, Consuela
or Cicero's conscience? The appellation was Quentin. Fina
lly. Pretious life bloode. Expensive batiment. Dying to fool
youngers flung her roses & all, outward bd. Tied up tight.

Think timely thyme. Shadowy motes of mean head diadem.
Chrysanthemum, Poppy, Tranquilizer divinity. The old one.
Veils over finery, bombs over the sea, soldiers de la sud. En
trance on the left, band of binies. Trackless citizenry, beet

riled up pistachery. A green cake, finally. Ukase, a decree, a
fierce metabolic. Blinds, wisteria, clears floors, etc. Enough
mind motion to set hollerin the body. Plashless fleshy boll.
The carillon decides deciduously to die. Hidden openly too.

Cobweb akimbo

Virginibus pueresque, Platon! Thin Mike,
duly impartitaed, all grandly delicieux, ha
the rooles of wrestling, our maker makes a
fuss soon enough, our lonely sub-nocturne
of whistley whispers, carbonifer, vertiginous
diff of deliquescence, rangers him & hears
fussies sad soulstarry with wind, Lamiae
coronum, sweet pimple, saucy pecs, who says,
he errs who hears a tiny tympani, beet red,
beneath a milkier trunk, tunc, sofas, moons,
mistress & more. Too know a dum locutor, mot
meditating verbies funk, trak, triple ace, a fragile
truce up lifted, pinks in a section of unibivalent
youngdoms due diadems devil, dry tanks o ale,
aloe us, halo, hallo nite, drop down Dives!

speck pecked

tween blu blink documentas, left to trip us up, tripe!
marx fleas he beard, how wintery, wise, whippetlike
not a bit. wipe us up, platoon. forge, frag, frak, lope
on n on big dogs. lianas, too lee ann thee wing,
speculatory ocean, blue willow cups. ming dynasty
four the sure. pling swansdown, fellowtravels
corporeal enfringement, haps, hoops, en
cour agment, augmented cour, knees floating, boating
to jello. pass onto junior clutch. status? fragmentary
at paramounting, delusionary as to the pangyrical part
headley, try instead englandery: encre de chine, fire
upon the studs, tea is bean servieted. what rivets too
documents? whist reeds, viola. sin ordinaire? without
ramby trembling brow to flow, art documents. pixie texts
wan fablier, lune, lang loverboy. oh those. lists parabola,
catalogs: singlefile instances, bullets, dots, swiss people.
categories distingue, inventorial screets, delineal rolls to
prove husbandary. fangled tripods hermetic, harmonic,
iambic alcmans, do something bout something. The role
and rile of, minimim mim oh florida, flor de
duh, save her fell lollies, perpetual crème rinse. caravel
of loneliness, sperando, placando un weaves wreaths
mouse, swaths, carpe diem per diem. scape savanarola
cede to savannah, sprint of spice, flange of tulle, speck!
ah, behind is flamenco, beginning caesura, keeping.
plateau, poetry suitsm think, corrigible beanie, we
ought out. potentiary penetentials, cascade midflower
mindflows smelt melt, vulcanic type. spock spekes to
us as doctor carnate, capatious heartbeat, aw in miniatory
combos, the coll. works of gnome c, last fleece treats,
exeunt fairies, bye bye, longtime.

Hammersmith, the end

What perfected, needed, foretold, is the wreck
Here is the mystic throng: ivory tiles, turnstiles
Someone hommaged. Beckham perhaps: High
Holborn, Covent Garden, Picadilly, explained
Is everything dirty? We must somehow know what
to do. Such beautiful lights.

There is no such place: parks forest wilderness
green masquerade of rest, let the jade ping until
your favors are delicate: sachets piled around
This neighborhood is turning French, in preparation
for tableaux

Single file fox gloves, the glamour!
we are back to scenarios not involving us
yet perfectly English and subterranean, en face
the typography will save us, incised or not
Isfahan, Bagdad I always
How did the war get in here again?

Notes

Untitled for now (after Sir Thomas Wyatt)
This poem is based thematically and rhythmically on Thomas Wyatt's "I Find no Peace" which is itself a translation of Petrarch's 134th Sonnet. In *Tottel's Miscellany* where it was first published in 1557 it was noted by the editor that the title was a description of the contrarious passions in a lover.

Travels without End (energy)
This poem is based very loosely on Pierre Reverdy's Voyage sans fin, and John Ashbery's translation of that poem.

The Last Letter to John Taylor
was published in the Sonora Review, no. 51 (2007)

Nuit de Varennes
This poem is a cento. The lines are taken from the following poems:

Frank O'Hara, "To Canada (For Washington's Birthday)"
Jane Cooper, "After the Bomb Tests."
Louise Bogan. "Evening in the Sanatarium."
Charles Bernstein. "Controlling Interests"
W. H. Auden, "Bones wrench, weak whimper, lids wrinkled."
John Ashbery, "Summer."
Walt Whitman, Elemental Drifts."
Frank O'Hara, "Poem (The fluorescent tubing burns…)."
John Milton, "Paradise Lost."
Marianne Moore, "People's Surroundings."

The Protestant Era
'The Catholic church, however, has manifestly been able to preserve a genuine substance that continues to exist, although it is encased within an ever hardening crust. But whenever the hardness and crust are broken through and the substance becomes visible, it exercises a peculiar fascination; then we see what was once the life-substance and inheritance of us all and what we have now lost, and a deep yearning awakens in us for the departed youth of our culture.' Paul Tillich, *The Protestant Era* (1948)

A Poem ending with certain unrelated lines by Byron
I would to heaven that I were so much clay,
As I am blood, bone, marrow, passion, feeling.
Because at least the past were passed away. .
Byron, part of an epigram originally written on the cover of *Don Juan*.
Love's a capricious power. I've know it hold
Out through a fever caused by its own heat,
But be much puzzled by a cough and cold
And find a quinsy very hard to treat.
                              Byron. *Don Juan*. Canto II, stanza 22.

The Literary Offenses of Fenimore Cooper
Some short phrases in this poems are from Mark Twain's famous comedic attack on
James Fenimore Cooper, published originally in *The North American Review* of July,
1895.

Nineteen Lines about Violets
Among the notable work of Swiss artist Thomas Hirschorn are his "perishable monu-
ments," created of ephemeral material from consumer packaging and discarded materi-
als such as plywood and tinfoil.. These monuments include work devoted to Spinoza
(Amsterdam, 1999), Gilles Deleuze (Avignon, 2000), Georges Bataille (Kassel, 2002)
and Antonio Gramsci (future project). I wish this poem was something more like them.

Poon and Playground
both are for John Jurayj, and were published along with images of his work, by Granary
Books in 2002. I am grateful to the amazing Steve Clay for this.

Chinas y Criollas
is for Blake West

Head in the Clouds
published in the *Sonora Review*, no. 51 (2007)

Lipstick for Halloween
for the ever loving and amazingly lovely Caroline Crumpacker, who else? It appeared
in *Sonora Review* no. 51 (2007)

Nightgown
published in *Pom2* issue 5 (2004), it is based on a poem by Edmund Berrigan, which
was in turn based on a poem by Magdalena Zurawaski

Aquarium
at least, is for Frances Richard.

Besoin de Need & Genealogical Rhapsody
The name of Olson's poem, is of course, "The Kingfishers"

Ornaments of the Red Professors
Francis O. Matthiessen, the author of, among other things, the classic *American Renais-sance*, taught at Harvard from 1929-1950. Newton Arvin, the author of, among other things biographies of Hawthorne, Melville and Whitman, taught at Smith from 1922-1963. Both were leftist in politics and homosexual and were victims of the homophobic and evil times in which they lived.

Untitled (Radio de dream)
is for Jane Cooper, the title in parentheses borrowed from her.

Cobweb amused
Many of the words, latin and otherwise in this
poem were taken from the Odes of Horace.
It was published in *Spinning Jenny* in 2007

About the Author

Rodney Philips lives in Tucson, Arizona. He is resposible for *Hand of the Poet: Poems and Papers in Manuscript* (1997) and *A Secret Location on the Lower East Side: Adventures in Writing, 1960-1980* (1998).

About Chax Press

Chax Press has been publishing books in Tucson Arizona since 1984. Recent works include books by Norman Fischer, Samuel Ace & Maureen Seaton, Leslie Scalapino, Charles Olson, Mark Weiss, Drum Hadley, fine letterpress chapbooks by Anne Waldman and Eileen Myles, and many more. We have published 138 books to date, and look forward to many more in the next several years. Please visit our web site at chax.org, and look for our books at the Small Press Distribution web site, *http://spdbooks.org*. Chax Press has received support from the Southwestern Foundation for Educational and Historical Preservation, the Tucson Pima Arts Council, the Arizona Commission on the Arts, and the National Endowment for the Arts, but the greatest part of our support comes from individual donors. To join our supporters, please visit our web donation page at *http://chax.org/donate.htm*.

TUCSON PIMA
ARTS
COUNCIL

Arizona
Commission
on the Arts

NATIONAL
ENDOWMENT
FOR THE ARTS